Ground Cover

Ann Pilling

Indigo Dreams Publishing

First Edition: Ground Cover
First published in Great Britain in 2015 by:
Indigo Dreams Publishing
24, Forest Houses
Cookworthy Moor
Halwill
Beaworthy
Devon
EX21 5UU

www.indigodreams.co.uk

ISBN 978-1-909357-96-9

British Library Cataloguing in Publication Data. A CIP record for this book can be obtained from the British Library.

Designed and typeset in Palatino Linotype by Indigo Dreams.
Cover design by Ronnie Goodyer from the painting 'A View from Welton, Yorkshire' by John Sell Cotman, reproduced by permission of the Bridgeman Art Library.
Author photo by Arthur Francis
Printed and bound in Great Britain by 4edge Ltd.

Papers used by Indigo Dreams are recyclable products made from wood grown in sustainable forests following the guidance of the Forest Stewardship Council.

in memory of

Elizabeth Bishop

Harvard 1972

Acknowledgements

I would like to thank the following people for their thoughts on some of the poems in this collection:

Dawn Bauling, Chris Considine, David Harsent, Ben Pilling, Joe Pilling, Thomas Pilling, Fiona Sampson and Tamar Yoseloff; also the members of Poets Meeting, London, Settle Poets and David Scott's Kendal Group.

Some of these poems have been published in Acumen, Envoi and Resource and have been included in the following collections: 'Distilling Life', 'Hildegarde, Visions and Inspirations' and 'Say Cheese!' They have won prizes or been commended in the following competitions: The National Poetry Competition, Torbay Open Poetry Competition, Cafe Writers Competition.

Other poetry by Ann Pilling

The Dancing Sailors (Indigo Dreams Publishing)
Home Field (Arrowhead)
Growing Pains (Smith/Doorstop)

CONTENTS

Ground Cover

It is always the same subject an artist paints,
his own experience of the world.

Keith Vaughan 1912 - 1977

Child

Julys I'd eat clover, take
its purple helmet head into my mouth
and suck its sweetness; scutch-grass,
chewed for its milky bead at the root end,
could cut like glass and fill the mouth with blood.
I liked the taste of it swilling round my teeth,
the citrus smell when a crumpled dock
rubbed away stings, but best
was lying face down in the grass to smell the earth
feel it come up to me like a slow animal
unfolding from the horizontal.

Today I stretch out in a quiet place.
Big after rain, the beck hammers the bridge and geese
swim round three sheep marooned on a little island.
This shadow on the grass, is it clouds or trees waving
or my first self, running over the fields to meet me?

Leitmotif

I have been here before
walking along a road like this, usually by torchlight,
looking for something lost

a cockerel, the gold drop
of an earring set with pearl,
somebody's child.

A high-up amber bead turns out to be
a marooned kitten's eye, some white rags
the remains of a dog.

My beam flits
moth-like over hopeful bushes
rests its wings then moves on.

These huntings
thread through my life, I am out most nights now,
my torch beam stronger, my ears and eyes
better pricked, not knowing what I look for.

Picnics

They will be back, the families, trailing across the sand
looking for somewhere to park themselves;
and the boys will run off towards the rocks
and the girls will sit in a circle and arrange things
and wine will be opened and something happy played on a radio
and the day will uncurl itself
and stretch out towards the horizon.

Then a mother will say *Where's Molly?*
(or Melanie, or Tim, or Holly)
and they will all leave the place and take off
like a flock of birds rising from the horizontal;
quite soon villagers will line the cliffs
like newspaper headlines.

For now, this raw spring day, an oyster catcher
fiddles about in the mud and two gulls squabble
over something we are too far off to see.

Crème Brûlée

Tap goes the spoon's beak
on sugared onyx making white webs,
splinters crack open, sink into a honey sea
and we suck sweetness.
Behind drapes, frost skins the water meadows
where she used to skate,
town child testing her heel on a grubby pond.

Ageing hostess now, serving a chic dessert, she watches
mouths shut and open , sees
juices dribble down chins,
itches, as her mother did once, to wet
the clean corner of a hanky with her tongue
and make all clean.

For George in Scotland

Today I think mainly of trees because on waking
after your night journey you whispered
'Trees' in a voice soft as leaves.

Then we were out on the grass and I saw
your stubby toes dig deep in its ancient softness
milking the earth. The crag
was Chinese White that morning, a slip of sky
caught on it like a blue hanky while the trees
stood sentinel for you at the jaws of life

Later through a long window we saw
rabbits. Taking my hand you uttered
'Peter' in your light leaf voice.

Half Term

This headlong field behind the house unrolls like a map,
unfurls like a sail and turns green ocean, its stone wall
the fret of regular waves; the beat of wind
takes up my inside beat which has quickened all day
as the road between us shortens.
The children are coming.

In his shed a man stirs reddle, each tupped ewe
will be daubed with it but they graze oblivious,
a gun-crack stilling them for a second
before they drop heads again. Towards dark
I wander out to inspect the lane, its camber is swelling,
it's a pregnant lane ready to split.

And I want to tell the world that the children are coming
that I'm waiting for their baggy cavalcade to trundle down the road
in a riot of dogs and cases.

Dusk closes, dimming the sheep
strung out across the fell like little lamps
too far-off for me to shout to them
I'm opening the gates!

Post Codes

Down here by the Cathedral in SW1
up there in DL8 below the Creamery
children charge round at break-time
on identical hard squares.

Their voices come to me like birdsong
fragmented leaves from plane trees
puffs of lambswool floating up to a dark fell
but they are caged, all gates
are padlocked, urban walls
festooned with wire and broken glass;
they can't play out any more.

Yet there are still fixed seasons
for hopscotch and skipping
and if town met country
they would eye one another across the asphalt
dawdle in opposite corners then join up,
running and bouncing and yelling
in the games people play.

Hackney Marshes

Boxing Day

The children zip ahead on shiny trikes
grannies swap Christmases, the marshes
unroll themselves towards a flat horizon.

It is very dead. The birds and butterflies
are pictures on tourist boards, a horse clops by
on a fraying rope, water moves like a slug.

This filter bed is as big as a swimming pool
and beautifully shaped, sloping inwards like a Japanese dish;
three rusting fish heads poke up through brown reeds.

Could they be shell casings, rubbish chucked here
after the Blitz when these levels rose ten feet
losing a Roman causeway to silt?

The marshes are waiting, like something ready to spring.
Grendel, Leviathan, all the dead of London gather themselves
with long limbs. The children look tiny against all this.

An Evening Walk
for Elizabeth Bishop

I could make wine from these late brambles,
the berries are intensely sweet
and tiny and curiously pointed, as if intent
on making a statement.

As the sun drops this water's panelled gold,
on its bed all the egg-shaped pebbles show clear
the big ones like melons, we watch
the current snag itself on a thin upright stone,
wrinkling the surface
as if someone's drawn a nail across it.
In a corner of the churchyard a lone grave, green-furred,
presses itself for warmth against a wall, we pass through
to the homeward meadow where the light's flower-soft
all the sheep tinged rosy. That rock in the middle
that jagged finger-post with the iron lump stuck in it
what is that rock? The remains of a gate? Excalibur?
I have noticed before
that the ewes always give it a wide berth.
Lower down , where the river makes big snakes,
four rabbits chase each other over their grazing grounds
in the lee of a grassy rampart, quite high
and pointed like those berries in the hedge.
The guide book says it's an ancient flood barrier.

Suddenly the smallest rabbit is left alone.
Can rabbits swim? What's happening
on the other side of that rampart? The setting sun
seals a composite image of meadow, stone and water.
But where to begin, which thread
To follow from here?

I'll go for the rabbits.

Helpston

At Grantham the train gathers speed
as if being sucked towards the capital through a straw
then a signal box flashes by in the middle of nowhere,
Helpston, where John Clare was born.

.
The land tilts slowly uphill
then suddenly drops, like waves breaking.
Pylons stride over it. What might he have made
of pylons and wind farms?

Nothing probably, he's more likely
to have stretched out on the ridged earth looking at beetles
or at what the crows were up to, he would have loved
the shape of these clouds

curvy and long like wallowing water beasts,
like fishes with fringey tails, like swans.
They were kind to him in the asylum. I hope he died
as Falstaff died, babbling about green fields.

Moss

has crocheted a rock pool against the walls
of this wide-hipped house, a single feather
has been embroidered on it and the stamp
of a small horse's hoof. Things must have been
left out in the cold when this place took its first stand
against oceans. I hear on the wind
the susurration of an ancient tide.

Starlings

The new birds glitter
crusted with gold and silver beads
sprayed over wings and breast
and fight for fat-filled shells and wrest
pickings from thrush and finch
and claim the battleground
inch by cantankerous inch.

The first years strut in rosy leggings,
bead patterns soften as they grow
to a full starling finish, sheeny purple
and green like oil on water; unimaginable
that these will ever get tired or old,
take on the full, dull black
of priestliness, or widowhood.

Young Owl

All I saw of the owl was a stain on a curtain
and under a table a feather curled into a ring;
it had come down the chimney into an unused room
and battered itself to death against the glass.

They had washed down the walls
scoured the floor of its shit and its blood
put flowers in a jug by the side of the bed
and I slept there

and dreamed that the mother was flying around the world
big as God
tearing flesh with her talons
calling for justice with a strangled cry.

I said to her *Such things happen, floods rise,*
entire generations are drowned, in one grief
are many agonies But the cry went on
till the world had become all owl
and the sky was black with its wings.

The Peach Tree

Ivy has spilled its crocketed green flowers
over the wall like a landslide, no wonder
the branch of this peach has all but broken away.

Through its rusting leaves a vine
has threaded black necklaces,
muscats little as beads but of great sweetness.

The ground is all amber, peaches
half a foot deep on the bleached grass;
wasps mosey about in the rottenness

miles from anywhere. I fill my mouth
with black and coral fruits,
pick ivy to root in a jar,

think of quiet lives quietly lived. No-one
applauds this swansong of the peach
or praises its harvest of all time.

Convent Garden

Silence falls slowly here
like milk poured from a pitcher
by a woman with parted lips

here where a fig uncrimps
five-fingered buds and the beginning fruits
swell on curved branches

where drenched alleys lead to nothing
but another straight walk or a stone saint
or a bench angled to look at leaf light on grass.

But something has passed this way
there are shiny brushings against a wet hedge
and the silence has an edge to it, like fine steel.

Copper

for M B

It has snowed. I bury my toes in the stob rug,
in scraps of skirt and old men's suits
that suck cold from the kitchen flags
and find a squirrel there, its belly
eaten away, its brush
curled round my foot in a caress;
all week we watched its brilliance in the garden
weaving its copper scarf through the bare branches.

I crunch my spectacles into my pocket.
to blind myself the only way I know
but seared on my pupils is its narrow profile
the mouth half open, paws
drawn up under the chin
and that small child's look of mild surprise.

When I carry it outside
its blood seeps through the cloth, the earth
is too hard for a grave so I mound snow round it
pat the top flat and smooth it like icing.

Three lads lark about in the next field
rolling snowballs down a long hill
that get bigger as they speed up. Half way down
they have to heave them over a ridge;
they're as big as hay bales when they hit the fence.

And I watch. Passing before my eyes
is everything that has ever mattered to me
in the death of this small thing which,
greedy for beauty, I lured close,
too cat-close, ignoring your warnings.

Friend of my life, let me weep.
Let me bury my face in your hair.

Shooting Party

Bertie shot a crocodile with eighty eggs inside her, bagged
four tigers and an elephant hacking off its tail, lunched
on twenty courses served on Indian silver.

Princes never shot round here, the likeliest kill
would have been Harker's bull.
Nothing bigger than a cat slunk by the river
where they fished for brown trout and the occasional elver.

It was always too remote for a royal visit
too poor for a shooting party, the requisite
large house not being close enough at hand
and when war came, to hear the crump of guns
too far inland.

Holiday Reading

A rat cooked slowly in a stock made out of animal glue
could be quite succulent. With their long teeth
horses tore thatch from cottage roofs but rejected
a mash brewed up from wood shavings.

Horse was good.
People ran from the shadows with knives and saws
before the beasts drew their last breath.
When it came to pets, neighbours made swaps,
You take my dog, I'll take your cat. The children
were sent to Babushka until it was over.
We are not told
how human flesh tasted.

Remembrance

The silence is too short.
It cracks before setting
while the church tower reels from a punch of eleven strokes
and birds fly out of crevices, arrowing
over the fields then drift about like burning scrap.
A band plays 'Valiant Hearts', six black-robed clergy
form a line of hunched-up crows
and a child steps forward cumbered with poppies
for her boy father; the mother holds back
like Niobe, all tears. In the crowd a face cracks
then another, and another, and another.

Babes in the Wood

Do you remember when we fell asleep after love,
your cheek still soft against my shoulder and my inside arm
milk white? Our sleep was dreamless then, a soft
fall into feathers on the breast of God, our faith a hard brilliant.

We wake today to rain hammer and the moan of wind.
Brown leaves twirl down in ringlets and a cat
unfolds itself from your knee-crook, wants downstairs,
where the dog howls in its confines.

Tortoise

I would like to go to sleep now. I would like
Daddy to come and put me in a stout carton,
fill it with straw and strew me with twigs and beech mast
so, when I drift away, I carry with me
good memories of the earth.

Sometime our pets would not wake up. One spring
I poked a stick in the hole where Lizzie's head was
and this pink dust came out. My sister screamed
but I poked harder till our father said
'Leave it now love, she's dead, we'll get another.'

He told us kind lies if our creatures vanished
while friends were minding them. I knew
that Frank from the prefabs had stolen Snowy,
while we were at Rhyl, and that Mrs Druce
let our dog run under the Number Seven bus.

Lies about women were harder.
'No woman, no affair, your darling mother's
my only love', he didn't know
she had shown me that letter in his overnight bag
and the poem, stuffed into a sock.

Turtles and elephants
live to be old because they pace themselves, attend
more thoughtfully to their condition
than small, fleet things, he outlived her
by thirty years.

Tuck me in tight,
let the soft layers
be good and thick.

Black Dog

I am not going to cry anymore because of my brain's black
it has happened before, it has happened many times before,
this hurl of my body down a long shaft
dropped into sizzling cold where I flail about
clanged under manhole covers but kept alive,
alive and twitching with probes
with my eyes stuck open, I had forgotten
the sheer physicality of this black place.

Even the demons had friends, even the demons
held grim little hands and sank together with defiant grins
but I am left alone with this black. They tell us
trauma is stored for ever in the body
and if they sliced me open they'd find black inside
as they did with miners and child chimney sweeps
prematurely dead.

The Armourer Comes for My Stepmother

He is taking away her armour piece by piece
grieves, gauntlets, helmet, cuisses. She has
no use for them now. He will
re-cut, melt down.

This recycling would please her;
there was always a hardness,
our early gifts for example, after the marriage,
would go into stock for her cleaners.

I envied her long hands, her gloves
fine as a skin, her long feet
in those luminous green shoes we marvelled at,
children, too frightened to open our mouths.

Now she stares long and hard at the cheese grater
wondering what it is for. Last night
she came into my room
sifting through my features for our long-dead father.

Yellow

I had forgotten how yellow was she said
but I can look again and she polished her spectacles
and put them in the fridge.

In time her lover took her to a plastic house
where all was immaculate
each surface scoured hourly.

When he kissed her perfect mouth
she rolled back her lips baring fangs
like something caught in a trap.

They dressed her in Aloine's clothes, all pink
a colour she detested and they cut off her hair
so it didn't get caught in things.

She loved the shiny rooms and the smiley people
her smile too got fixed
except when her lover came

with his sheaf of yellow lilies.
Each week she said *You are very persistent,*
teeth readied for his departing kiss.

The Remains

There was nothing on her the hospital said, no watch, no rings,
and the dress she wore had to be cut away. She brought
nothing into this world and she took nothing out.

I walk through her treasury, oils, bronzes,
a zebra's head hammered in tin and a man
sweeping leaves. Rings big as humbugs, pearls

tangled with corals and hair. I see the inheritors
drape their uncrumpled necks,
waggle fingers through.

I must box it all up, make lists, but my hands
have shrunk into claws. I am iced
with death's terrible loneliness;
and it feels like looting.

Bethlehem

So we arrived at Bethlehem
knee-deep in litter and blind with tourists
where Mary lay once on an earth floor
and squirmed and pushed until he slithered out
with a cow licking him into shape.

She gave birth in the back of the cave
because it was warmer
the animals hunkered down shoulder to shoulder
only the baby
lay on his back in the straw
gazing through a hole in the blackened roof
at one unfocussed star.

Mount Tabor

The trees lean sideways here, their bony trunks
stripe the sky and the spongy tops
of the Aleppo pine cool its hot blue

and everything gleams and is glittery
the gravel, the big stones,
the very heat is white.

If they were people these slanting trees
would throw up their hands and reel back
and turn and hide in a crevice of the rock
till the glory of the Lord had passed by.

Magic Man

Don't tell me how it's done –
the egg behind the ear
that started as a penny in his hand,
the lady sawn in half that takes the stage
cool and unharmed.

Don't give the game away –
the rabbit in the hat,
the scarf he tosses into empty air
and turns to two white doves, the burning book
untouched by fire.

Keep something back –
a country woman's womb
swelled by unhuman seed, water to wine
a curtain ripped, graves yielding up their dead
an empty tomb.

The Lamplighter

Today more swallows notch the wires, clouds
turn solid suddenly, as if programmed,
heat is a memory.

On a new tree
six apples glimmer under a weak sun
leaves shrivel and drop.

I am regretting this escape to Greece
planned that month of the long rain
when rivers tore up fields and cables.

When I come back
blinds will have been pulled against the year
I will have missed the slow steal of winter

the lamplighter with his long pole
cycling from path to path
every night earlier; this sudden
snapping on of the lights will seem too quick a death.

American Trucks

I looked at them on the highway between Cleveland and Erie
at the hang of their chubby wheels
at their shiny square faces,
unfazed by the hugeness they pull, these trucks
are picture-book Daddies, children
would climb all over them.

The space between the driver and his long load
is a box tall enough to stand in, chair, stove, bed,
somewhere to piss,
when we stopped for gas
I saw family photos and nudes
a sheet of wisdom from the Shawnee tribe
Seek to make your life long and of service to your people
Give thanks for your food and for the light of morning

It recalled an old movie. In it, most weeks,
a man drove his truck to the south ,
his wife packed him off with kisses and bread
a soft-faced man, short, with a little domed head.

For a year, halfway down, someone waited for him
at the Honey Child Inn
they made love but he always looked sad
till one day she did not wait,
bored or discovered or dead
no-one said. I still see the sadness,
the look on his face, the stunned
drive home to the wife, in his cab pictures
of her and the child and the dog which he never took down.

It's at night I see truckers, steadying the reins
of their benign chariots, ploughing

down long unvaried furrows, working
through guilt or desire as the big engines thrum, freed
to consider the life of the mind
and I push through my pillows to join them
I want to climb in, stow
away with them go
to the light and the end of the light
to the sea and the sea's end.

Shetland

All night the engines thrummed under our heads
and we came to the island
and stepped out of the boat into fresh clean skins
to a wave of cranes and ships like shoe boxes
to the red and yellow houses of the oil men
and brilliant torn skies
to beaches spread with caster sugar sand
where guillemots chequer ledges and great skuas
idle and plane across soft moor
and bog cotton shakes from the fingering of the wind.

Binoculars

Through these, a blackened stick
piercing the sea like a gloved finger
becomes the neck of a diver and that buoy,
glossed by the sun, turns into a seal's head.
Through these, I observe the antics of puffins
how one inches up sheer cliff
to join its mate. I am watching
nothing distasteful or private simply
the routine lives of others;
but it feels like spying.

I'd like to go back
to that spine of land on Shetland
and hurl these lenses from east to west,
from the North Sea into the Atlantic.
For now, I could daily
bend the knees of my heart
to those quiet creatures.

Birders

In June the Inner Farne's all beaks and chicks
all trippers; a man on the board walk
shoves me aside with his telescopic lens.

I hate all this staring, how all of us ogle
the nests at ground level, no wonder
the terns shit on our heads

look villainous as we shuffle past but move
with tenderness among the feathered bees
that are their children.

Puffins do mouth to mouth feeding,
stuff in the sand eels
that fringe their beaks like combs.

We feed in Cuthbert's chapel, grit
on the altar, the fine panelling
from Durham warped and split.

A gale scoops up the litter,
no boat back. We are stuck,
battered by the saint's fury
and his birds.

Lowry People

You can see how they became sticks,
burnt matchsticks blackening the streets like rooks,
here too on Spitall beach his back-lit couple
merges and lengthens while their dog
draws one straight line across the sand
turning into the stick it races for.

He watched how the sea rears up
half spends itself, falls back then comes again;
his nightmare was that it would keep on coming,
the ultimate thinning of his people.

Eden

after John Burnside

What did God mean when he put
two people in a garden and in the middle
that supreme tree
and the snake of a river
to water it and a back lane
where he could spy on them
in the cool of the day
letting frogs fill the silence?

Why didn't he provide
a shed for these people
and a little fence
give them neighbours?
His revenge was terrible
angels at all four corners
with flaming swords to protect the Tree of Life.

Their error was minor
everyone gets hungry at times
but they were thrown
into the wilderness for sharing an apple.

Eden became a dream,
from then on there was only mud and labour,
Eve spawned children like tadpoles
while from his harsh fields
Adam watched her grow fat
and found another woman.

Watering

Come into the garden, I'm watering. Let me show you
my shiny green hose with its snake-like markings, the brass
fittings that clench the tap, the five-way jet

but she's late for her lover and turns on the path
Cool she says *Cool, as the young say*
though she has no young. Mine are scattered and my mate gone.

Here I stand, Lord of Creation, with my new device.
No-one's coming, I could water
all day and all night,
I could wash the moon out of the sky, I could walk naked
with my hose between my legs, soak the baked soil
like a man does, I am in control.

Then a joint breaks near the tap and I'm knocked sideways
slither in mud, fall back into a huge rose,
hit my head on the wall while the water spews over me
unleashed, raw. I can taste my own blood.

Queen Lear

I'm old and I want to go naked.
If I lay out for weeks in blistering sun this skin
that puckers like cling-film when I draw a nail across it
might thicken and darken, I could be a seal,
in a cold climate I might grow fur,
I could be a bear. Hefty and waistless,
the bear and the seal are poetry in water.

Pulling two stockings as far as my knees
takes an hour and I have to rest after, some days
I can't make my bed, my fingers
have twisted like thorn twigs, this torpedo body
is not the willow limbs men worshipped once.

So it's *Off, off, you lendings! Come; unbutton here.*
Fetch me a big sea. Grand pups and grand cubs
swim with me now.

January

Putting away takes longer now because we are tired.
It is weeks before the baubles are boxed up
the tree dragged out, lines ruled
through names in the address book

and eleven months from now it will resurface
this paraphernalia that marks our passage.
Simpler is that slice of moon on the calendar clock
the sundial with its spine of winter shadow.

How long the Princess and Curdie took crossing the earth
is not recorded but this I do remember:
his hair was white before their journey ended
and round her eyes crows' feet had gathered.

Pictures at an Exhibition

i Red Tricycle

It hangs narrowly between window and wall.
The picture itself is narrow, so is the runner
on which the tricycle stands; off a corridor
doors loll half open, the small chariot
presides over a stillness.

Viewed from a distance it slews
slightly to the left, its skewed wheels
suggest two eyes that peer hopefully
towards the nearest door.

It is too quiet now. They have gone
to their schools and to their universities,
there is no one to play with. The red runner rages
pours down in spate till it hits the bottom of the frame
taking the tricycle with it.

ii Blue on Blue

I am easy with this
any of these blue lozenges
might be a pool I could swim in.

If the wall behind is north
then they all point west
snub-nosed like porpoises

and from a distance
start blurring into one another
only the darkest stay separate.

This is the way to go
west with these lovely shapes
always a dark one leading.

Notes

Shooting Party (page 25)

'Bertie', King Edward VII, made a state visit to India in 1875, when still Prince of Wales. Details of his shooting triumphs were published in The Times, to the anger of Queen Victoria.

Holiday Reading (page 26)

The book in question was 'Leningrad, Tragedy of a City Under Seige', Anna Reid 2012.

Yellow (page 32)

From the film 'Away from Her', 2006, starring Julie Christie and Gordon Pinsent, about the effects of Alzheimer's Disease upon a marriage, based on the short story 'The Bear Came over the Mountain' by Alice Munro.

Queen Lear (page 46)

Off, off, you lendings! Come; unbutton here. King Lear, Act 3, Scene 4.

Pictures at an Exhibition (page 48)

'Red Tricycle' by Naomi Pilling b. 1973, private collection.

'Blue on Blue' by Martin Creed b. 1968. Hauser and Wirth, London 2010 'Mothers', work no 1065.

About '*The Dancing Sailors*':

'The opening poem 'Life' amazes being so full of life; it's an attenuated, confident selection of surprisingly apt details. There's nothing metaphysical, no fancy concepts...an interesting collection, modest, deft, oblique. Pilling glances at everything, moon, stars, wonder, creatures, countryside. So – a 'nature poet'? But there's no saccharine pastoral. It's lively stuff, strong stuff, even macabre. It's very good to meet Pilling's work. Most of her poems say something in a world where so many poems say almost nothing at all. Hooray for that.'
R. V. Bailey
Acumen

'In the title poem, *The Dancing Sailors* Pilling speaks of suicide, "your slacks bulgy with pebbles", Woolf in the Ouse and "Van Gogh's final cornfield" with a fragility which is intensified after reading her note at the back of the book. This is a collection of recollections, memories, and the journey of the human spirit.'
Abegail Morley
The Poetry Shed

'The poetry of Lancashire-born Ann Pilling is a constant reminder to us all that the very transitory nature of a lifetime's existence is, in its truest sense, a virtual celebration of all we hold most dear, and that not only, therefore, does it merely encompass that essential period between birth and death, but also provides a shared heritage of treasured, poignant remembrances for one's surviving loved ones, despite the inevitability that, by its very nature, Time, in the meaningful generality of its essence must ever move on. This appealing collection, with its multifarious insights into those seasonal, locational and circumstantial changes in Ann Pilling's world is well worthy of a place on any poetry lover's bookshelves.'
Bernard M. Jackson
Reach Poetry

Indigo Dreams Publishing Ltd
24, Forest Houses
Cookworthy Moor
Halwill
Beaworthy
Devon
EX21 5UU
www.indigodreams.co.uk